"This is a book without peers. Kerrie Hide has retrieved the voice of lamentation as a necessary moment in the authentic spirituality of women going through separation and divorce. Their experience, too easily marginalized by the church and its pastoral ministers, finds a more than engaging guide in *A Woman's Healing Song*. Hide journeys through the precincts of powerlessness, anger, loneliness, and emptiness, while combing the writings of Julian of Norwich to discover how these moments yield to the transforming power of God's unconditional love. The meditations on gospel texts centered on women, her halting prayers, her suggested spiritual exercises, and Julian's wisdom as a polar star—all combine for an uncommonly mature book of Christian spirituality.

"Kerrie Hide helps women navigate the Scylla and Charybdis of discernment and decision making to claim empowerment as freedom and creativity. Her interpretation of women's experience through the lens of contemplative prayer gives birth to a resurrection life lived playfully. I urge pastors, counselors, and even men going through separation and divorce to read this book and to discover how the unraveled yarn of life's suffering can indeed be reknit into even stronger cloth."

George Kilcourse
Author, *Double Belonging: Interchurch Families and Christian Unity* and *Ace of Freedoms: Thomas Merton's Christ*

"What a healing book this will be for any women going through a crisis. It is aimed straight to the heart of healing through prayer and meditations; it benefits the healing process, which can also be a time of spiritual growth.

"The healing song can be sung alone or in a group and would be very powerful for women not only when going through a divorce but through any crisis of mid-life, such as losing a loved one through death. It is a new way of praying during the difficult grieving process when we need God the most, but may also be angry toward God.

"Kerrie Hide has shown us how to allow God into our lives during this tough time so that real healing and growth can occur. A Woman's Healing Song can help raise a woman's self-esteem, which is always at its lowest point after a divorce."

Kathy Brewer
President, Board of Directors
North American Conference of Separated
and Divorced Catholics

"Kerrie Hide invites the woman who has experienced the trauma of separation and divorce to look to the God-within-self for strength and courage during the grieving process. Her prayers give voice to what are often jumbled and confused emotions. The activities provide helpful suggestions that enable the woman, in her journey from darkness to light, to make healthy decisions for herself. This book is truly an invitation to emotional and spiritual growth—a process that leads to wholeness and the courage to risk."

Dorothy J. Levesque, Executive Director
North American Conference of Separated
and Divorced Catholics

"With the divorce rate running at about forty percent of marriages, divorce has become in North America a plague spreading loss, grief, regret, and despair for what might have been. Given the structures of our society, no one suffers more in divorce than women. To them Hide sings an empathetic, compassionate, and empowering healing song. Blending scriptural stories of women, the unmatched visions of Julian of Norwich, an a faithful woman's prayerful insights, the Song invites women to recognize, to own, and to begin again from one reality that remains forever unchanged: God made me, God loves me, God preserves me. In the future, when I counsel both women and men of divorce, I shall have a new piece of advice for them: please read *A Woman's Healing Song*."

Michael G. Lawler

"A woman who has faced the end of a marriage that she believed in undergoes an interior assault on her shattered expectations, her new and strange loneliness, and her sense of being abandoned, even by God. The challenge of putting together the Humpty Dumpty pieces, to become whole and restore balance to her life so that it makes sense again is formidable. She needs help, particularly in forging a new relationship with God. Hide's compassionately written book provides this help, particularly by introducing hurting women to a magnificent friend, Julian of Norwich, whose revelations put a new spin on how and why we can trust that God, our Father/Mother, loves us and will lead us to know joy again."

Antoinette Bosco
Author, *A Parent Alone*
Executive Editor, *The Litchfield County Times*

"The pain of divorce is more than emotional; it touches the spirit as well. This work is an invitation for spiritual renewal and growth. Hide has given women a gentle guide for their spiritual re-awakening. It is an important work that offers women the ability to seek transformation; changing the pain of loss into an opportunity for new strength.

"Through scripture, prayer, reflection, and mediation, Hide invites her reader to rediscover the God who is companion, lover, and friend. Her book is a journey into a greater intimacy with one's self and one's God. It can be used for individual healing, spiritual discovery, or even among small groups for discussion. Hide offers a feminine perspective that can touch the souls of men as well."

Rev. James A. Heneghan
Chaplain, North American Conference for Separated
and Divorced Catholics

A WOMAN'S HEALING SONG

Prayers of Consolation
for the
Separated & Divorced

KERRIE HIDE

XXIII
TWENTY-THIRD PUBLICATIONS
Mystic, Connecticut 06355

Twenty-Third Publications
185 Willow Street
P.O. Box 180
Mystic CT 06355
(203) 536-2611
800-321-0411

ISBN 0-89622-535-6
Library of Congress Catalog Card Number 92-60754

Contents

A WOMAN'S HEALING SONG

Introduction

This book grew out of sharing the stories of women going through separation and divorce. Each story is unique in detail, and each brings its own sense of grief, loss, regret, and failure. This series of meditations is presented to help women reflect during this time of grief and stress so that the major transition involved in divorce or separation may become instead a time of great blessings and spiritual growth. The readings and activities provide opportunities for women to undertake the tasks of grieving, by encouraging them to acknowledge their brokenness, to be attentive to God's presence in their lives during this period of suffering, and thus to experience God's healing love.

Divorced women are among the most powerless members of society because they have lost their previous identity, often have low self-esteem, have had to face up to failure, and cope with a change in financial status. In this fragmented state, depression, despair, fear, and self-rejection can manifest themselves. In contrast, divorced women may also experience that they are powerful because initiating divorce may be the first time they have made a decision that results in freedom for themselves and perhaps for their children. By acknowledging this fragmentation and allowing God into their lives at this difficult time, real healing and growth can occur. Conscious self-appraisal and an appraisal of former ways of living can lead women to come to know themselves better and thus come to know God more intimately.

The purpose of *A Woman's Healing Song* is to encourage women to take responsibility for their grieving, reassuring them that although the process of grieving will take time, it is natural and healing will come. It offers hope, recognizing that no matter how painful the mourning may be, women can place themselves in God's hands and healing will occur. It gives authority to women's experience, suggesting that they are being called to a new way of being Christian, which will bring them dignity and acknowledge their equality with men.

Role of Prayer and Reflection During Times of Grief

Prayer during times of grief can provide support and nourishment, help us realize that God is with us and loving us during our most painful moments, and help us perceive more specifically what God is trying to do during this time. It can sustain us when there seems to be nothing else left. When we are in crisis, our old ways of living and praying come up for re-evaluation and we discover that we are being called to deeper intimacy with God. As we reflect on who we are and on our relationship with God, we realize in a new way that at the root of our being we are in contact with the infinite power of God, and that it is only God, the source of life and love and grace, who can help us to heal.

As we journey through the grieving process, we encounter fears we have not met before. We begin to struggle and search and reach out as we long to experience God's healing. We may find prayer difficult because of the exhaustion that encompasses everything, because of the intensity of the pain we experience, and because of the frightening emotions evoked. Perseverance in this difficult period, however, will lead to growth in relationship with God, self, others, and the universe. God is abundantly generous to those who wait out the process of healing.

These meditations are a vehicle for grieving women to be faithful in listening to God in their very depths, so that the gentle, unassuming voice of God may guide them and fill their lives with love. They encourage women to see their entire life as prayer.

Method

The sessions are designed to encourage women to set some time aside to be with God and to engage in active listening in open, honest friendship. They encourage the sharing of stories: the women's own stories, the stories of Jesus with women, and the story of Julian's experience with and understanding of God. The use of the imagination is encouraged to enable women to enter into the details of their story and the story of God's revelation so that insights may be illuminated and their meaning grasped. The images and stories offered in this volume were chosen to bring out the value of women's experience and to encourage women to reflect upon it so that it may become prayer.

There is an emphasis on feminine images of God to remind women that they too are made in the image of God. The Scripture passages depict Jesus' encounters with women calling them forth to healing and empowerment.

Women are encouraged to live out, as their own, the biblical story of Jesus empowering women. Creative activities have been designed to invite women to reflect on their own experiences so they can more readily see the transforming power of God working in their lives. The activities are designed to build up women's self-esteem so that they may realize that this world needs to be enriched by what they have to offer. Symbols are used to help women gain insight into their relationship with God and to help them express what they know deep down within, but cannot express in any other way: God has become involved in their lives and their experiences have lasting significance.

Who the Book Is For

This book is designed for Christian women who have experienced divorce or separation. It may be used by those in spiritual direction and counseling, or by those who work in retreat settings. It is also written for individual women to use as a guide in self-direction and prayer or for groups of women who may wish to have some direction for prayer, discussion, and shared activities.

Julian and the Separated or Divorced Woman

Julian plays a dominant role as a model and guide for grieving women because her life was so united to God. It is affirming for women to realize that great women have gone before them who expressed their relationship with God in ways that relate to women's experience. The language and symbols Julian uses to describe her intimate relationship with God are rich in everyday imagery; this can help women see and touch and taste the presence of divine love in their lives. Julian gives us insight into the meaning of suffering, since her theological reflection is grounded in the passion of Jesus. Her writings draw women into Jesus' suffering so that they may, in their suffering, be healed and share fully in Jesus' joy. She shows us that Jesus is with us in our suffering and that we are healed when our wounds are open to the penetrating love of God.

Suggestions for Using This Book

Women are encouraged to find a sacred space where a comfortable atmosphere can be established. Lighting a candle or some incense or playing some reflective music can help set the scene. Keep in mind the sacrament of the present moment. In this moment you encounter God.

Each section begins with an opening prayer. The first time you use the readings you might want simply to read the passages. The next time you might complete some of the activities. Continue going back to the meditation until you feel ready to move on. You may wish to return to the meditation after you have completed others.

At the end of each chapter, activities are suggested to help externalize what is felt deep within. Many of them have a contemplative aspect, encouraging women to use everyday activities as a way of enjoying a relationship with God. The meditations invite women to delve into the core of their relationship with God, to experience themselves rooted in God in endless love.

> For our soul is so deeply grounded in God and so endlessly treasured that we cannot come to knowledge of it until we have knowledge of God, who is the creator to whom it is united. But nevertheless I saw that we have, naturally from our fullness, to desire wisely and truly to know our own soul, through which we are taught to seek it where it is, and that is in God. And so by the leading through grace of the Holy Spirit we shall know both in one; whether we are moved to know God or our soul, either motion is good and true. God is closer to us than our own soul, for he is the foundation on which our soul stands, and he is the means that keeps the substance and

the sensuality together, so that they will never separate. For our soul sits in God in true rest, and our soul stands in God in sure strength, and our soul is naturally rooted in God in endless love (pp. 288-289).[1]

To grieve is an invitation to participate in the paschal mystery.

Julian of Norwich

Julian was born in 1342 and died some time after 1416. She was an anchoress, a person who kept herself in religious seclusion, attached to the church in Norwich, England. Her portrait is set against a background of poverty, pain, and death. She lived in the time of the plague, or Black Death, when life was bitterly disintegrating before her eyes. She was surrounded by illness, natural disasters, and unemployment, which led to fear and hopelessness. Preachers were constantly referring to the wrath of God. Julian, however, experienced nothing but the tender love and mercy of God. It was out of her experience of suffering that she came to understand just how much God is moved and anguished by the pain of creatures, how loved we are, and how we can be filled with hope and affirmation. When she fell into sickness so severe as to seem at the point of death, she was counseled to look upon the crucifix. It was after this that she experienced the passion of Christ, an experience that changed her life. She received a deep knowledge of the love and healing compassion of God and decided to describe this experience in her Showings.

Julian the Woman

Like so many women over the years, Julian describes herself as a simple, unlettered creature. Historians are unsure of the level of her education, but whether educated or not, her work reveals the insights of a gifted woman. Her experience of God was different from the experience of men who had written about God. She had the courage, fortunately, to trust her own experience and to share it with others. Julian in her day would have been treated with suspicion, and could even have risked being burned at the stake as a witch. However, she protested against convention in her quiet way because she knew that her insights came from God. She overcame her feelings of being ignorant, weak, and frail because she experienced the all-encompassing love of God. She writes:

> But because I am a woman, ought I therefore to believe that I should not tell you of the goodness of God? (p. 135).

She encourages all women to be true to their experience of God.

Julian's Writings

Julian wrote two accounts of her Showings, the short text written shortly after her experience, and the long text which contains the reflections and insights gained from 20 years of reflection. She teaches us the importance of reflecting on experience. She uses symbols, images, and parables and the everyday language of Norwich to translate her experiences into theological concepts. She challenges us to express our relationship with God in our own everyday language.

Her rich images and sensual detail come out of the experience of a woman deeply united to God. Her writing reveals her as a saintly woman, a gifted mystic, and a distinguished prose stylist. Her language is particularly earthy and feminine, giving us a glimpse of a side of God not often presented in image and story. She teaches us how close God is in a time of crisis.

Julian's Image of God

Julian reveals a deep understanding of God. She knows that God is very "accessible, familiar and courteous" (p. 196). She describes God in intimate terms: our maker, our keeper, our lover, and our protector, reminding us also of the kindly, homely nature of God. God is not a distant, stern judge, but a companion who suffers with us. Julian's God is relational, whom she constantly experienced as being in relationship with all creation. She describes the loving unity expressed in the Trinity in this way:

> ...the Trinity is our maker, the Trinity is our protector, the Trinity is our everlasting lover, the Trinity is our endless joy and bliss, by our Lord Jesus Christ and in our Lord Jesus Christ (p. 181).

> And so I saw that God rejoices that he is our Mother, and God rejoices that he is our true spouse, and that our soul is his beloved wife. And Christ rejoices that he is our brother, and Jesus rejoices that he is our savior (p. 279).

Relationship with Jesus

Julian sees her relationship to Jesus as a pathway to God. She develops an intimate relationship with him, coming to a realization that Jesus is at one with us. As she reflects on the passion of Jesus, she gains great insight into the meaning of suffering. In Jesus she sees the mystery of God revealed. Jesus is her best friend, her homely and loving confidant, her brother, her sister, her mother:

...and the second person of the Trinity is our mother in nature and in our substantial creation, in whom we are founded and rooted, and he is our mother of mercy in taking our sensuality. And so our mother is working on us in various ways, in whom our parts are kept undivided; for in our mother Christ we profit and increase, and in mercy he reforms and restores, and by the power of his passion, death, and resurrection he unites us to our substance (p. 294).

Julian offers us images of Jesus—companion, mother, and lover—that can bring support and comfort to grieving women.

Julian's Teaching About Prayer

Julian, a deeply prayerful woman, teaches us that God longs for us to pray. God expects us to recognize the divine presence in the ordinary occurrences of our lives. She reminds us that our whole lives, and not just certain moments, are a continuous prayer growing out of God's absolute love for us. From this understanding, we can appreciate that God is with us in all our daily tasks, no matter how trivial. She playfully tells us that our bodies are like a well-made purse:

When the time of necessity comes, the purse is opened and then shut again, in most seemly fashion. And it is God who does this, as it is shown when he says that he comes down to us in our humblest needs. For God does not despise what God has made, nor does God disdain to serve us in the simple and natural functions of our body, for love of the soul which he created in his own likeness (p. 186).

She also points out that God is with us in our suffering so

that the pain we experience due to the loss of our partners can become a prayer, even if we *feel* that God is far away. When we feel alienated, we can reflect on the life of Jesus and see ourselves in him. We will receive insight whether this is revealed in darkness or with clarity of vision.

Julian describes six ways of prayer, which she does not see in a hierarchical manner as many of her contemporaries did, but rather as something that encompasses all of life. We would experience these ways at different times in our lives.

The first way she describes as "seeking" (desiring). This is the natural yearning we have for God to be the center of our lives.

The second, "asking" (beseeching), is our need to ask, or even plead, for the things we need. When we are grieving we need to plead with God to be with us as we suffer.

The third way of prayer is "thanksgiving," a time when we are grateful for our lives, both the positive and negative aspects, and enjoy being in relationship with God, thanking God for our blessings.

The fourth way is "working" prayer. People at a time of grief come to understand in a new way Julian's experience of "working." This is a time when we need to persevere with prayer, even though it is difficult to pray. Julian explains that God accepts our prayer no matter how we feel. She reassures us that this difficult, painful, dry time won't last. Eventually we will experience the fifth way.

The fifth way is the prayer of "beholding," which, to Julian, is the whole purpose of prayer: to be united to God in love.

The sixth way, Julian describes as the prayer of "enjoying," the fruit of contemplation, the time when we simply enjoy God.[2]

Julian offers us great encouragement to continue praying

even in the darkest moments. Even then, we can develop our relationship with God afresh. She shares Jesus' words:

> For he says: Pray wholeheartedly, though it seems to you that this has no savor for you; still it is profitable enough, though you may not feel that. Pray wholeheartedly, though you may feel nothing, though you may see nothing, though you think that you could not, for in dryness and in barrenness, in sickness and in weakness, then is your prayer most pleasing to me, though you think it almost tasteless to you. And so is all your living prayer in my sight (p. 249).

Julian encourages us to move ever more deeply into the goodness of God and all creation and never to forget that no matter how we may feel, "Love is our Lord's meaning"; we are loved.

Relevance for Suffering Women

Julian's Showings is a timeless vision that can be an inspiration to women today. She reminds us that we are created for love and that our whole life is a prayer before God. Her Showings have layer upon layer of insight into the human condition of suffering and the place of God in this suffering. They draw us into the suffering of Jesus so that we may feel at one with him and thus experience his joy more fully. She helps us to realize that healing is possible, that our experience of pain may lead to a transfiguration in our lives. Her vision and understanding were often sought after by women who were suffering because of discrimination, poverty, or frequent painful childbirth. Margery Kempe, a contemporary of Julian's, left a record of the support Julian gave women. In her autobiography she loudly proclaims Julian's wisdom.

Julian's timeless work can still be a source for spiritual guidance to women who are grieving. Reflecting on her wisdom can enlighten our understanding of our own experience. She speaks clearly and poignantly to "all who would be saved" (p. 192), reminding us that "God wishes us to know that he keeps us safe all the time, in sorrow and in joy." God is with us when we grieve, longing for us to find peace again:

> For it is God's wish that we do all in our power to preserve our consolation, for bliss lasts forevermore, and pain is passing, and will be reduced to nothing for those who would be saved. Therefore, it is not God's will that when we feel pain we should pursue it in sorrow and mourning for it, but that suddenly we should pass it over, and preserve ourselves in the endless delight which is God (p. 205).

Our God of Comfort

God is always with us, holding and loving us in times of great loneliness and turmoil.

Opening Prayer
Compassionate One,
come and embrace me.
I have need to feel you at one with me.
Like the widow, I feel I have given much
And now I feel empty and alone.
Help me to give freely, to let go
of past ways of loving.
Open my eyes, my ears, and my heart
to your words of life.

The Word of God
As Jesus looked up and saw rich people dropping their gifts into the chest of the temple treasury, he noticed a poor widow putting in two small coins. "I tell you this," he said, "this poor widow has given more than any of them; for those others who had given had more than enough, but she, with less than enough, has given all she had to live on" (Luke 21:1-4).[3]

Reflection

Notice this poor widow. Perhaps she has spent many years alone or perhaps she became a widow only recently. She knows what it is to have to begun to build a life by herself without another for support. She was able to be generous and appreciate her life as a gift, even though she was grieving and felt like one of the poorest members of society.

Like the widow, we need to acknowledge our life and appreciate it as a gift so that we may offer our marriage as it was with all its joys and sorrows generously to God. This is not easy, because no matter what our story, each of us has loved our husbands at one stage in our lives. We may have the precious gift of happy memories. For some of us, moments of peace and contentment were fleeting; for others, the moments endured. Some of us feel angry and bitter about the way we were treated; others are just sad. Some of us fled a destructive situation, because of tragic, violent, and unbearable circumstances; others were deserted against their will. Whatever the details of our marriage story, God is with us in love as we seek to reconcile the past and be at peace in the present.

Now because of our separation we are challenged to a new way of living, to discover what it means to be a woman alone. This will mean coming to terms with great loneliness. We must search for our identity, confident that God will be with us as we undertake a re-evaluation of our lives. God enters the human condition on the side of the poor, the fragile, the rejected, the lonely, and is generous, never ceasing to bestow abundant love unconditionally.

The widow in the parable offers us a model. This woman, although appearing fragile on the surface, has a power of her own: she has discovered that God surrounds her in love and gives her power to be herself. She was not afraid to take the risk to offer her life's story generously to God. She not only reminds us of our own story, but she also symbolizes what God is like. God is abundantly generous, caring deeply if we are oppressed, depressed, or exploited. God will surround us in love until we are able to live life peacefully again. May we join this poor widow, Julian of Norwich, and all women who grieve as we embrace our past, acknowledge our broken dreams, and creatively build a brighter future.

Praying with Julian

Julian also knew what it was like to be alone, since she lived a life of solitude as a hermit. She teaches us that loneliness can eventually lead to peaceful solitude if we allow God to enter this painful place. In her solitude she came to experience God as the great comforter who encloses us in goodness.

Julian's Wisdom

For as the body is clad in the cloth, the flesh in the skin, and the bones in the flesh, and the heart in the trunk, so are we, soul and body, clad and enclosed in the goodness of God. Yes, and more closely, for all these vanish and waste away; the goodness of God is always complete, and closer to us, beyond any comparison (p. 186).

God wishes us to be enclosed in rest and in peace (p. 229).

When we feel like the widow, Julian assures us that we can rely on God to be constant in love for us. God is trustworthy and will never desert us, even though we are broken and seemingly unlovable. The fact that we are human means that we are utterly immersed in God's love, just as a fetus is enclosed in the womb. We are held warmly in the embrace of our maker, no matter how difficult and unbearable our circumstances might be.

Julian uses the metaphor of clothing to describe what this love means. We can allow the cloth that is enfolding us—divine love—to become our skin. In this sense we are transformed into the goodness of God. Like a mother, God nourishes us with goodness. Let us keep this constantly in mind as we seek to offer our experience of loss to God.

Suggested Activities

•Take some time to become still. Listening to some reflective music may help.

•What does it mean to be alone? Perhaps it is when we feel really alone, when we've had our world shattered, that God moves in and surrounds us in love, just as the body is clad in cloth and the flesh in the skin. This can be a time we can grow much closer to God. Spend some time imagining God surrounding you in love.

•Reflect on your loneliness. See if you can find an image to capture this feeling. It might feel like a deep dark hole, or being lost in a crowd, or being exposed with no protection. Stay with this image. What does it feel like inside? Ask God to enter this feeling. Feel God's love surrounding you.

•What is the coin (past ways of living) you are finding most difficult to let to go of?

•Who are the people you have to let go of? Your partner, a child, children who don't live with you any more, in-laws?

•Perhaps you could ask this widow to help you to adjust to your loss. Allow her to walk with you. Perhaps she will place her cloak around you as you struggle together.

•Choose a symbol to represent your loss and place it in a special place where you can reflect on it. Lay it on some cloth as a reminder that God is surrounding this painful memory in love.

Closing Prayer

God of grievers, giver of hope,
we know you enclose us in your goodness,
even when we feel abandoned.
Give us the power of this widow
to give you the treasured
and painful moments of our lives.
We know you will hold them gently.
We remember that we are
soul and body,
clad and enclosed
in your goodness.

(2)

Finding Companionship

Because God calls us to intimate companionship, we become pregnant with God's love.

Opening Prayer
O God, who fills my life with love,
become more present to me.
As Mary and Elizabeth listen
to each other's experience of God
and affirm each other,
may I remember the women
who have given me life.

The Word of God

Mary set out and went as quickly as she could to a town in the hill country of Judah. She went into Zechariah's house and greeted Elizabeth. Now as soon as Elizabeth heard Mary's greeting the child leaped in her womb and Elizabeth was filled with the Holy Spirit. She gave a loud cry and said, "Of all women you are most blessed and blessed is the fruit of your womb. Why should I be honored with a visit from the mother of my Lord? From the moment your greeting reached my ears the child in my womb leaped for joy. Yes, blessed is she who believed that the promise made her by the Lord would be fulfilled" (Luke 1:39-45).

Reflection

Mary and Elizabeth teach us that women can be empowered to have life and freedom, to be supportive companions who listen to each other's experiences of God. Through this sharing they gain greater insight into the meaning of God's presence in their lives. At first they found God's presence disturbing; now, in their pregnancies, they are radiant with expectation. The earlier days of shock and perhaps sickness are over; now, at this time of the visitation, they joyfully await the gift of new life. Mary and Elizabeth empower each other, affirming that the love of God has filled their lives. They remind us that this love is also available to us, even though we are experiencing shock and sickness because of the divorce. Mary and Elizabeth remind us not to lose hope, that things will change. Elizabeth, after all, had to wait for years to have her child.

Praying with Julian

Julian also came to understand in a profound way that God's promise of love would be fulfilled. Because of her experience of pain and her growing realization that God was with her in this pain, she was able to listen compassionately and support those who came to her with their troubles. She reassured people that God has filled their lives. She reassures us:

Julian's Wisdom

For God is everything that is good, as I see; and God has made everything that is made, and God loves everything that he has made (pp. 191-192).

God has made us and loves us and fills our lives with love and will never remove her hands from her works. She continues:

And therefore the blessed Trinity is always wholly pleased with all its works; and God revealed all this most blessedly, as though to say: See, I am God. See, I am in all things. See, I do all things. See, I never remove my hands from my works, nor ever shall without end (p. 199).

Julian's words remind us that God is our constant companion. God never leaves us, even if we feel that she has gone. When we feel most alone, God's hand is with us constantly, gently filling our lives with love and encouraging us to keep growing. God is always with us, longing for us to become closer companions.

Suggested Activities

•Recall a woman who gave you life in some way. As you reflect, describe her to yourself. Imagine yourself having a conversation with her. You may find it helpful to write or draw the conversation.

What do you want to tell her?
What do you want to ask her?
What is her response?
She brings you a gift. Open it.
Reflect on how this this gift is going to give you life and freedom.
Pray a blessing for this woman whom you love.
Ask her to journey with you as you grieve the loss of your partner.[4]
You can repeat this process with other significant women in your life.

•Find an article in the newspaper about a woman who has been hurt and pray for her.

•Is there someone you know who could help you unburden yourself when life seems difficult? Perhaps you might be able to find a spiritual companion who can walk the journey of recovery with you.

•Eventually you will be able to support other women. Do you know a woman who needs someone to talk to? Spend some time with her and affirm in her the realization that God is present in her experiences.

Closing Prayer

Thank you, God, for the women
who have gone before me.
May I not forget the wisdom they teach me.
Thank you for the women
in my life today.
May we support each other
to recognize your presence in our lives.

3

Seeking Forgiveness

When we know we are loved, it becomes easier to forgive.

Opening Prayer

Courteous God, sometimes I feel like such a failure;
I have so many regrets.
Help me to forgive myself,
to forgive those who have hurt me,
especially my partner.
Help me to experience your forgiveness.

The Word of God

The scribes and the Pharisees brought a woman along who had been caught committing adultery; and making her stand there in full view of everybody, they said to Jesus, "Master, this woman was caught in the very act of committing adultery, and Moses has ordered us in the law to condemn women like this to death by stoning. What have you to say?" They asked him this as a test, looking for something to use against him. But Jesus bent down and started writing on the ground with his finger. As they persisted with their questions, he looked up and said, "If there is one of you who has not sinned, let him be the first to throw a stone at her." Then he bent down and wrote on the ground again. When they heard this they went away one by one, beginning with the eldest, until Jesus was left alone with the woman, who remained standing there. He looked up and said, "Woman, where are they? Has no one condemned you?" "No one, sir," she replied. "Neither do I condemn you," said Jesus. "Go away and sin no more" (John 8:1-11).

Reflection

God loves us enough to draw us closer, no matter what our situation may be. We see this love expressed in the story of the accused woman. It was of little importance to Jesus what her past had been. He could only meet this woman in love, openly challenging those who were judgmental. Sometimes, as divorced people, we may feel exposed and have experienced the prejudice of others. Sometimes shame overwhelms us and we begin to engage in self-doubt and self-rejection. Julian reminds us not to do this. Our courteous God never burdens us with guilt, but offers us love and support instead so that we may become whole.

Praying with Julian

Julian gained the insight that we are forgiven by a loving God. She received Jesus' assurance that sin and all its afflictions are only temporary and that God's love will embrace all things eventually.

Julian's Wisdom

And this was the beginning of the teaching which I saw at the same time, whereby I might come to know on what manner he looks on us in our sin. And then I saw that only pain blames and punishes, and our courteous Lord comforts and succors, and always he is kindly disposed to the soul, loving and longing to bring us to his bliss (p. 271).

And when we have fallen through weakness and blindness, then our courteous Lord, touching us, moves us and protects us. And then he wants us to see our wretchedness and meekly to acknowledge it; but he does not want us to remain there, or to be much occupied in self-accusation, nor does he want us to be too full of our own misery. But he wants us quickly to attend to him, for he stands all alone, and he waits for us continually, moaning and mourning until we come. And he hastens to bring us to him, for we are his joy and his delight, and he is the remedy of our life (pp. 334-335).

Julian was fully aware of the tension between God's love and the mystery of suffering and evil, and was fully convinced that God does not cause this suffering. The closer we are to God, the more we are aware of the need to forgive and be forgiven. Julian teaches us not to be afraid to shed light on our mistakes, but rather to bring all our infirmities before God where they will be surrounded in love and healed.

Suggested Activities

• Take some time to ponder God's words and Julian's wisdom in your heart.

• Do you feel exposed and accused like the woman in the story? Remember that this story is written with a patriarchal bias. Does this story of prejudice resonate in your life?

• Reflect on the symbol of the stone. What are the stones you are carrying? Collect some stones, remembering Ezekiel's prayer that our hearts of stone may become hearts of flesh.

• Perhaps emotions such as anger and bitterness arise when you begin to reflect. Hold these emotions gently, remembering that unrecognized, unintegrated infirmities can become enduring attachments that can prevent us being in harmony with God. Attachments can be neutralized when we openly acknowledge them. Simply acknowledge how you feel and place this before God. Remember that good friends can be brutally honest with one another.

• Remember Jesus' words: "Neither do I condemn you." Say these words over and over as a mantra.

• Do you think it would have been difficult for the woman to forgive the stone-throwers? Whom do you find it difficult to forgive?

• Whom do you need to forgive? Yourself, your partner, children who don't understand how you feel?

• Remember Julian's words, "Our courteous Lord comforts and succors, and always is kindly disposed toward you." Write these words decoratively in your journal.

Closing Prayer
God, who fills the hungry with good things,
teach me to listen
to ponder
to accept
to forgive.
Hold me as I struggle
to hold together the conflicting feelings
that overflow in me:

the fear
the loneliness
the despair.
Help me not to forget
the joy
the light
and the peace.
And that I am your joy and delight.
Hold me, gentle one.

(4)

The Crown of Thorns

It is often the thorns that reveal how deeply we are loved and how deeply we love.

Opening Prayer

The crown of thorns is there before me,
made up of each broken dream in my life
The thorns are sharp, penetrating.
Will I own this crown, claim it, make it my own?
O God, you are with me.
To you, my love, I give this fear.
To you, my peace, I give this grief.
To you, the only source I need,
I give my life, my broken life.
Journey with me.

The Word of God

They dressed him in purple and, plaiting a crown of thorns, placed it on his head (Mark 15:17).

Reflection

When we are in the midst of grieving, anger, hurt, frustration, fear, self-rejection, and doubt all become present in a jumbled mess. If we can acknowledge this fragmentation and place it before our loving God, healing will occur.

Praying with Julian

Julian's revelation of love is beautifully captured in the "precious crowning of the thorns." This was her first revelation and the basis for all her other revelations.

> This is a revelation of love which Jesus Christ, our endless bliss, made in sixteen showings, of which the first is about his precious crowning of thorns; and in this was contained and specified the blessed Trinity, with the incarnation and the union between God and man's soul, with many fair revelations and teachings of endless wisdom and love, in which all the revelations which follow are founded and connected (p. 175).

The crown reveals layer upon layer of meaning. "In Julian's garland there is an unconscious intertwining of what pervades her entire teaching—the intertwining of joy and sorrow as are flower and thorn."[5] It represents for her Jesus' suffering and victory over death, and also the insight she gained through her own suffering. It is a reminder for us not to lose hope, because eventually through suffering with Jesus we become his crown. She came to understand that Jesus will bring "us up into heaven and make us his crown and his everlasting bliss" (p. 220). Now the crown of suffering becomes the crown of love and victory over suffering.

Julian reminds us that no matter what our feelings may be, we are understood and crowned in God's love. Jesus embraced the crown of suffering and love. He experienced all the pain that we feel and is now ready to crown us in compassion. He knows how difficult it is to embrace the crown.

Julian's Wisdom

The blessed body was left to dry for a long time, with the wrenching of the nails and the weight of the body; for I understood that because of the tenderness of the sweet hands and the sweet feet, through the great and cruel hardness of the nails the wounds grew wide, and the body sagged because of its weight, hanging there for a long time, and the piercing and scraping of the head and the binding of the crown... (p. 207).

Julian also speaks of a second crown, a garland of blood.

And then I saw that it was so; what adhered to the crown began to dry and lose weight, so it was surrounded, as it were a crown upon crown (p. 208).

The drops of blood flowing from Jesus' head also became a crown. This flows into the story of women. These drops are to be found in a woman's most precious center. They become the gift that enables us to give life. This second crown also describes the suffering of members of the church. It reminds women in grief that we are not alone in having our lives turned upside down. Jesus is suffering with us, as he also was "hanging up in the air as people hang out a cloth to dry" (p. 208). "The passion has become compassion."[6] Jesus suffers along with us and we suffer along with Jesus. We share Jesus' crucifixion and resurrection, neither without the other. The crucifixion was not the vision that continued. Jesus was transfigured into incredible beauty. Jesus bonds himself to us and teaches us how to transform ourselves from a preoccupation with suffering to an inexpressible joy and a sense of absolute assurance that God is with us, loving us.

Suggested Activities

•Play some reflective music to help you center.

•When Jesus was grieving, he was cloaked in purple. Choose a color that represents how you feel. Draw or paint a picture using this color. Reflect on how you feel while you are doing this.

•Make a list of the things you consider you have lost since the separation began.

•As you identify your losses, make your own crown of thorns, choosing a symbol that is significant to you to make the crown. As you embrace the painful story of your marriage ending, make a section of the crown. You can add another piece to your crown as you continue grieving. If you don't feel like finishing it, leave it unfinished. It may take years to finally embrace all the anger, loss, pain, and suffering you feel.

•Write down all the feelings you experience associated with your loss. They may be contrasting such as fear, hope, regret, anger, betrayal, rejection, frustration, love, failure, terror, to name a few. Attach your feelings to the crown of thorns. Ask God to help you acknowledge these feelings; then gently hand them to Jesus as you attach them to the crown.

•Are there any things that you thought you might have lost that you still have? List these. Could these become strengths?

•See if you can also find a symbol that signifies a glimmer of resurrection.

Closing Prayer
My tears create a crown of love.
The thorns, though sharp,
actually support a sweet-smelling rose.

In my despair I realize that you are with me,
my beloved God.
Saturate my thorns with your healing blood.
You are my life.
Become my source, my longing, my peace.
Let me not forget that resurrection—new life—is possible.

5

Journey to the Tomb

When we enter the tomb, we realize that we are held lovingly in God's womb.

Opening Prayer
God is with me when I am homeless
powerless
faceless.
God longs for my wholeness.
My gentle one, where are you now,
as I journey to the tomb?
I used to know you were with me.
Let me feel your presence once more.
I wait, gently hoping.
As I enter this tomb, embrace me, clothe me,
Surround me in your love.
Become my home, my power, my face, my voice.
Transform me with your healing love.
May I become one with you.

The Word of God
Mary stood outside the tomb weeping, and as she wept she peered into the tomb, and saw two angels in white sitting

there, one at the head and one at the feet where the body of Jesus had lain. They asked her, "Why are you weeping?" She answered, "They have taken my Lord away, and I do not know where they have laid him." With these words she turned around and saw Jesus standing there, but she did not recognize him. Jesus asked her, "Why are you weeping? Who are you looking for?" Thinking it was the gardener, she asked, "If it is you, sir, who have moved him, tell me where you have laid him, and I will take him away." Jesus said, "Mary!" She turned and said to him "Rabbuni!," which is Hebrew for teacher (John 20:11-16).

Reflection

Because Mary visited the tomb she met Jesus. She did not run away from her sorrow, but rather went to this sacred place to spend some time grieving. She needed to weep in order to be healed. In the tomb, which reminds us so much of the cycle of life from womb to tomb, Mary gazed on the tender face of Jesus and recognized that he was "her maker, her keeper, and her lover," the one who would heal and empower her. She realized that Jesus did not want her to stay in the tomb, but was challenging her to go out to the world again. She teaches us that we have to spend some time grieving before we can create a new fuller and richer life.

The crisis of separation and divorce is catalyst for a transformation in our relationship with God, ourselves, and others. It is a time of pain, of despair, and of letting go of our old, familiar ways of knowing, loving, and laughing. It is now our time for weeping.

This confrontation with loss leads us to journey to the tomb as Mary did, to discover God's presence deep within. Something inside has died and we must attend to its burial.

Often we feel so afraid to enter our hearts because we have lost our peace and stillness. We feel deeply hurt and emotionally damaged. The old image of ourselves that we used to recognize seems no longer present. We are not sure who we are. We are in a void, lost, bewildered and alone. We can't feel the touch of God. Our body seems shattered, desperate to feel God's touch, and yet there seems to be no God to strengthen us, no one to hold in this time of desolation. God has left us alone.

We have not lost hope, however, but tentatively step forward, searching desperately, ready to take the journey that Jesus knew so well, the road to Calvary. We stand crushed with hands reaching out, grasping. We trip and fall, and yet we continue. Our silent God is there in the pain, weeping, loving, holding us as we seek to reclaim and fashion our image that is in God. God's vulnerable love reaches out to us. God gently calls us forth, longing for us to realize that we are held lovingly during this painful time.

Praying with Julian

Julian knew the experience of weeping, as she, like Jesus, lay for three days and nights, not expecting to live. This was her time of being in the tomb. During this time she encountered divine love, which, like our clothing, wraps and enfolds us, and also brings healing. As we journey to the tomb to grieve, God wraps and enfolds us.

Julian's Wisdom

I saw that he is everything which is good and comforting for our help. He is our clothing, who wraps and enfolds us for his love, which is so tender that he may never desert us (p. 183).

As Julian became even more conscious of God clothing her in love, she wanted to share this understanding with others. She reminds us that we are enclosed in God's warmth, love, and security. She describes how welcoming her maker, her keeper, and her lover is:

> With a kindly countenance our good Lord looked into his side, and he gazed with joy, and with his sweet regard he drew his creature's understanding into his side by the same wound; and there he revealed a fair and delectable place, large enough for all mankind that will be saved and will rest in peace and in love. And with that he brought to mind the dear and precious blood and water which he suffered to be shed for love (p. 220).

In our divorce or separation, Jesus invites us to be enclosed by him, to feel secure in a place of nurture so that we can freely weep. In this we experience Jesus' motherhood, his womb, a place of healing where resurrection becomes possible. As we realize that Jesus' story and our broken story are so similar, we are awakened to a new way of living, recognizing that in our darkest moments we are actually being held in God's womb. Our experience of nothingness engages us in the paschal mystery, and resurrection can begin. Julian continues:

> For the almighty truth of the Trinity is our Father, for he made us and keeps us in him. And the deep wisdom of the Trinity is our mother, in whom we are enclosed. And the high goodness of the Trinity is our Lord and in him we are enclosed and he in us. We are enclosed in the Father, and we are enclosed in the Son, and we are enclosed in the Holy Spirit. And the Father is enclosed in us, and

the son is enclosed in us, and the Holy Spirit is enclosed in us, almighty, all wisdom and all goodness, one God, one Lord (p. 285).

As we birth from God's womb, we recognize that God is also in our womb. Like Christ, we are left with the possibility of being clothed in the love of God so that we may embody fullness of life.

Suggested Activities

• Take some time to become completely still in mind and body.

• Reread the passage from John and ponder these words in your heart. Imagine that you are at the tomb of Jesus. Your experience of separation or divorce has led you to encounter feelings similar to those of Mary Magdalene. It is now time for weeping. Now your profound loss is surfacing. As you sit in this void feeling torn, lonely, and forsaken, begin to realize that Mary and Jesus will bind your wounds and wrap your body in burial cloth. As they do this, feel their healing touch. Recognize that in your grief you are actually surrounded in love. You are being held in the womb of God. At first you might feel abandoned, and actually you are abandoned in God. This tomb is a safe place for you to return to whenever the grieving cycle returns to despair.

• Decorate the tomb in patterns that remind you of your story.

• Show Jesus those parts of yourself that seem most shattered and torn. Allow him to touch the broken, bleeding, raw areas of your heart. Allow him to bind them with his love.

• Like Mary, spend some time weeping. When you feel like crying, welcome your tears. Stay with these tears and reflect on the gift they give you.

•When we weep, an avalanche of emotions comes. As they come, remember that all of these are being wrapped in God's love.

Closing Prayer
Let us say Julian's words over and over as a mantra:

In the name of the deep wisdom of the Trinity
who is our mother,
in whom we are enclosed,
in whose womb we are nourished,
we ask for healing.
Enclose us in your love.

$$\left(6\right)$$

Created in God's Image

Women's images of themselves are often in need of healing.

Opening Prayer

O God, teach me to recognize my gifts,
to be proud of my story and my experience.
Teach me to recognize my own wisdom.
Come, O wisdom, lead me to goodness.
Teach me to value my life here and now.

The Word of God

While they were on their way Jesus came to a village where a woman named Martha made him welcome. She had a sister, Mary, who seated herself at the Lord's feet and stayed there listening to his words. Now Martha was distracted by her many tasks, so she came to him and said, "Lord, do you not care that my sister has left me to take care of the work by myself? Tell her to come and give me a hand." But the Lord answered, "Martha, Martha, you are fretting and fussing about so many things; only one thing is necessary. Mary has chosen what is best. It shall not be taken from her" (Luke 10:38-42).

Reflection

Martha personifies a vulnerable, caring woman who never had time for herself; she was constantly concerned for the hospitality and comfort of others. As women, we are often socialized into being helpers, placing our own needs last. It is important, however, that we make time to nurture ourselves, especially during a time of loss, so that we might grieve. This is not merely selfish, but is quite essential if we are to grow as individuals and in our relationship with God and others.

In Luke's portrait of Martha she is unaware of her own inner beauty and is constantly worried and busy. Jesus confronts her lack of confidence, reminding her that she too has a right to sit with him and talk. Martha reminds us that even though we are burdened with many daily tasks, we are also called to spend time with Jesus, so that we may realize we are made in God's image. To have no confidence and to be anxious and troubled with so many details is a common experience for overburdened women who live alone, or alone with children. We feel we have all the responsibility for so many tasks. Jesus calls us to share these burdens with him, to let go of stereotyped images of women, and to become fully ourselves. In Jesus a just humanity can exist. Jesus calls us to human liberation.

Within each woman is the impassioned call of God. God longs for us to realize we too are made in God's image and likeness. Kathleen Fischer[7] gives insight into how we can begin to appreciate that we are made in this way. She points out that growth in Christian self-image has three dimensions. First, we must pay attention to images that reveal the self, especially in its deeper aspects. We must begin to notice the beautiful, authentic parts of ourselves that make us "woman." Second, we must be honest about the destructive parts of ourselves, acknowledging these so that healing and the transformation of inadequate or destructive self-images can occur. Many of these images would be the feelings of inferiority that many of us experience. Third, we must discern and follow God's call in our life story, remembering that God is at work in all of these processes as we mature into the likeness of God. The divorce experience gives us the opportunity to re-evaluate our image of self and to establish a lifestyle that will foster self-confidence, independence, and growth.

Praying with Julian

Julian tells us that God does not want us to be miserable and to have a poor self-image, but to realize that we are a reflection of God's love. She uses the image of the knot to describe how preciously knitted to God we are.

Julian's Wisdom

> Therefore [God] wants us to know that the noblest thing that he ever made is mankind, and the fullest substance and the highest power is the blessed soul of Christ. And furthermore, he wants us to know that this beloved soul was preciously knitted in him in its making, by a knot so subtle and so mighty that it is united in God. In this uniting it is made endlessly holy. Furthermore, he wants us to know that all the souls that will be saved in heaven without end are knit in this knot, and united in this union, and made holy in this holiness (p. 284).

Sometimes, though, we forget that we are made in the image and likeness of God and dwell on our unworthiness, feeling like a poor laborer.

> Outwardly he simply dressed like a laborer prepared to work, and he stood very close to the Lord, not immedi-

ately in front of him, but a little to one side, and that on the left; his clothing was a white tunic, scanty, old and all worn, dyed with the sweat of his body, tight fitting and short, as it were a hand's breadth below his knee, looking threadbare as if it would be worn out, ready to go to rags and to tear. And in this I was much amazed, thinking: This is not fitting clothing for a servant so greatly loved to stand in before so honorable a Lord. And, inwardly, there was shown in him a foundation of love, the love which he had for the Lord, which was equal for the love which the Lord had for him (pp. 272-273).

When we are so close to God that we are knit in God's knot, we must remember the words from John's gospel that we are called to be "no longer servants but friends" of God (John 15:15). For Julian, the servant stands for all of humanity, for Adam who fell into the earth of misery, and for Jesus who fell into Mary's womb. God gives birth to the new Adam, Jesus, who picks up all humanity with motherly love. Separation and divorce initiate a dramatic about-face where our lives and our visions are altered. When this upheaval occurs, we feel like the servant, worn and tattered. We feel that we have fallen "into a dell" and are greatly injured (p. 267). Often, we feel like the servant who fell because our self-image is tied to our husband's. We spend such a long time living for and looking after others that we don't really know who we are. Bridges, in his study of times of transition, quotes a woman:

My self-esteem as a woman and as a person was all tied up in his reactions to me. I didn't lose a husband. I lost my way of evaluating myself. He was my mirror. Now I don't know how I look any more.[8]

Julian stresses, however, that there can be a positive side to this fall. We are led to realize that just as Mary's womb brought forth the life of Jesus, our Lord will bring forth life in us:

> [God's] great goodness and his honor require that his beloved servant, whom he loved so much, should be highly and blessedly rewarded forever, above what he had been if he had not fallen, yes, and so much that his falling and all the woe that he received from it will be turned into high, surpassing honor and endless bliss (p. 269).

Wisdom, goodness, and strength are offered to all. As a result, we may appear outwardly broken and powerless but this is not lasting. God comforts and assists us, offering us internal power, a foundation of love that can result in external power. God offers us love and through this love we can begin to discover who we are in our own right, as single persons.

Suggested Activities

•Take some time to become completely still.

   •How would you describe yourself?

   •How do you think God would describe you?

   •List the qualities you like about yourself and name the gifts that you feel you can share with others.

   •Read the story of Martha again. Do you find yourself identifying with Martha? What are the qualities in her that you admire? Where do you think growth lies for her? What can you learn from Martha?

   •What are the things that worry you most? Are you worried about your children? Tell Jesus how you feel. What does he reply?

•Think about who you are now and see if an image comes to mind. Choose an image to describe yourself. Look carefully at the feelings that surround this image. Draw these feelings. Reflect on the image to gain insight into who you are and what is going on within you. Remember that being in touch with yourself helps you to be in touch with God.

• A mandala is a drawing of seven concentric circles that can be used as an aid in prayer. Draw a mandala using symbols and colors that represent your relationship with God. Make this as elaborate or simple as you wish. Reflect on what this mandala says about your self-image and your relationship with God. Take this to Jesus, remembering that you are loved just the way you are.

Closing Prayer

Healing and all-loving God,
Today I have reflected on the story of Martha,
a woman you loved deeply.
She was a nurturer,
a woman of prayer,
of witness,
a woman who served
and listened to you.
You called her friend and you loved her.
You enriched her life and she enriched yours.
As I struggle
to bring together the disparate strands of my story,
breathe gentleness and strength into me.
Guide me in my search
for wholeness and reconciliation.

Give me the courage
to allow my hidden strength to surface,
to risk new ways of living,
and to respond to your call.
Help me to be gentle with myself
as I struggle to get to know myself better.

7

Discovering Our Images of God

During the crisis of separation and divorce, women often discover that their image of God begins to change.

Opening Prayer

O silent one,
I feel so empty and alone.
Come, fill my emptiness.
Birth in me.
Reveal your self
that I may love you deeply,
and come to wonder at
your unfathomable ways.

The Word of God

He was teaching in one of the synagogues on the Sabbath, and there was a woman there possessed by a spirit that had crippled her for eighteen years. She was bent double and quite unable to stand up straight. When Jesus saw her, he called her and said, "You are rid of your trouble," and he laid his hands on her. Immediately she straightened up and began to praise God (Luke 13:10-13).

Reflection

Although crippled, this woman had not the confidence to be herself. She was always trying to please others in order to be something she was not. This was weighing her down. She felt helpless and hopeless, colorless and drab. Life had been humorless, always a worry. Where was God in all of this? She wasn't sure. Perhaps God was reflected in all the men she knew. One thing she thought she knew was that God wasn't reflected in her life story. Jesus changed all this. He recognized her beauty the minute he saw her. He didn't pass her by, but stopped and lovingly touched her. He knew she was troubled, and he understood. Almost instantly change began. She realized that her image of God had not been accurate. God was not distant, unapproachable, but deeply interested in her life and the lives of all women. She began to realize that God was actually present within her. Jesus recognized that. She still carried her grief, but now she knew it could be transformed into something more beautiful. She knew that she had new ways of discovering life and God—and living both to the full.

Praying with Julian

Julian uses a variety of images of God to give us insight into how much God loves us. The hazelnut, one of her most famous images, gives us insight into her relationship with God, our relationship with God, and God's relationship to the world. As she reflects on this little item, she comes to understand that the whole universe is brought into being through the love of God. God is creator, protector, and lover.

Julian's Wisdom

And in this he showed me something small, no bigger than a hazelnut, lying in the palm of my hand, as it seemed to me, and it was round as a ball. I looked at it with the eye of my understanding and thought: What can this be? I was amazed that it could last, for I thought that because of its littleness it would suddenly have fallen into nothing. And I was answered in my understanding: It lasts and always will, because God loves it; and thus everything has being through the love of God.

In this little thing I saw three properties. The first is that God made it, the second is that God loves it, and the third is that God preserves it. But what did I see? It is that God is the Creator and the protector and the lover (p. 183).

Julian describes how small and seemingly insignificant the hazelnut is, and yet it is held lovingly in God's hand, being constantly surrounded in love. The hazelnut captures the image of a seed in a womb. This frail little thing stands for all that has been made. Its roundness, a symbol of unity and perfection. Its seed-like character reminds us that it has the potential to grow into a tree and produce more hazelnuts. It has the potential for life and goodness. The hazelnut has contrasting qualities. The outside shell is hard and difficult to penetrate, yet given the right environment it can be separated by a shoot. Inside the shell is something fragile and precious. We are like the hazelnut in so many ways with our layers of protection, yet inside there is something beautiful, a reflection of God. God is now offering us an environment where we can grow so that like Julian nothing can separate us from our creator. The hand surrounding the hazelnut is extended to grieving, troubled women to help us discover new insights into our relationship with God so that we may feel protected and nourished and therefore believe that we are signs of God in our world.

Suggested Activities

•Take some time to become completely still.

•Reread the passage from Luke. Imagine you are the women being touched by Jesus. Tell him about the loss you are carrying. What does Jesus reply? Feel Jesus' touch. Feel God's presence in your body and helping you gently endure your loss.

•Reread the story of the hazelnut and reflect on how you feel in relation to God. As you reflect on your experience as a separated or divorced woman, take this newly discovered self to God. Feel God surround this self in love. Just like the hazelnut, experience yourself in God.

•Look through Scripture and find some images of God as a woman (e.g., Isaiah 42:14; 49:15; Psalm 131; John 16:21; Galatians 4:19; Romans 8:22).

•Reflect on your image of God in childhood. What was your image of God while you were married? What is your image of God now? See if there have been any changes in these images. Choose some hazelnuts or another symbol that gives insight into your life in relation to God and make a design in a prominent place to remind you that you are constantly held by God.

•Use Julian's words as a mantra:

God made me.

God loves me.

God preserves me.

God is the creator and the protector and the lover.

Closing Prayer

Tender God,
as Julian reflected on the hazelnut
lying in the palm of her hand,

she came to an understanding
of the gentle and all-embracing love
you have for even the littlest creation.
Hold us as we struggle
to own the painful parts in our story.
Open our eyes to new glimpses of you.

8

Contemplate God in Everything: Prayer During a Time of Loss

Our way of praying may change during the grieving process.

Opening Prayer

Tears
wet salty
eyes swollen
empty.
Breath
sobbing
shaking
And yet in despair I am loved.

The Word of God

One of the Pharisees invited Jesus to a meal. He went to the Pharisee's house and took his place at table. A woman who was living an immoral life in the town had learned that Jesus was a guest in the Pharisee's house and she had brought oil of myrrh in a small flask. She took her place behind him, by his feet, weeping. His feet were wet with her tears and she wiped them with her hair, kissing them and anointing them with the myrrh. When his host the Pharisee saw this, he said to himself, "If this man were a real prophet, he would know who this woman is who is touching him, and what a bad character she is." Jesus took him up: "Simon," he said, "I have something to say to you." "What is it, teacher?" he asked.... Then turning to the woman he said to Simon, "You see this woman? I came to your house: you provided no water for my feet, but this woman has made my feet wet with her tears and wiped them with her hair. You gave me no kiss, but she has been kissing my feet ever since I came in. You did not anoint my head with oil, but she has anointed my feet with myrrh. So I tell you, her great love proves that her many sins have been forgiven; where little has been forgiven, little love is shown." Then he said to her, "Your many sins are forgiven." The other guests began to ask themselves, "Who is this man that he can forgive sins?" But he said to the woman, "Your faith has saved you; go in peace" (Luke 7:37-40, 44-50).

Reflection

In a time of grief our old way of praying often becomes unsatisfactory. The loss of a way of communicating with God, though at first painful and frightening, may lead to a richer, more intimate mode of communication. If we have relied on "saying prayers," we may now find ourselves called to more meditative or imaginative prayer. The imagination is a more adequate communicator for sharing pain, confusion, anger, and hurt. Nemeck and Coombs described this transformation:

> In meditative prayer one thinks and speaks not only with one's mind and lips, but in a certain sense with one's whole being. Prayer, then, is not just a formula of words

or a series of desires springing up in the heart; it is an orientation of our whole body, mind, and spirit to God in silence, attention, and adoration. All meditative prayer is a conversation of our entire self with God.[9]

While we are grieving, all our emotions are at their rawest, as we see in this story of the weeping woman. When upset, we are moved to our deepest levels, often feeling desperate. When we've been used to a close physical relationship with someone, we feel empty and deprived of touch, once this closeness has gone. Sometimes we feel afraid of the raw quality of our feelings. Jesus invites us to share this pain with him. He accepted the woman touching him, feeling her tears on his body. Madelaine Birmingham, who has listened to the stories of many grieving people, reminds us that our feelings, all of them, can be messages from God, that God can work in and through all feelings, including sexual feelings.[10] Our feelings of being deprived of touch can leave us empty enough to allow Jesus to touch us at the very center of our being. When we are touched deeply by Jesus, healing can begin.

Praying with Julian
Julian's writing about her prayer contains much sensual detail. She does not see Substance and sensuality (the spiritual and the physical) in opposition to each other but complementary. She came to understand:

Julian's Wisdom
...that our sensuality is founded in nature, in mercy and in grace, and this foundation enables us to receive gifts which lead us to endless life. For I saw very surely that our substance is in God, and I also saw that God is in our

sensuality, for in the same instant and place in which our soul is made sensual, in that same instant and place exists the city of God... (p. 287).

Julian encourages us to pray using our emotions, our senses, our sensuality. Using our normal human way of expression can help us become more intimate with God.

And then we shall all come into our Lord, knowing ourselves clearly and wholly possessing God, and we shall all be endlessly hidden in God, truly seeing and wholly feeling, and hearing him spiritually and delectably smelling him and sweetly tasting him (p. 255).

Julian realizes how important prayer is, reminding us that it "unites the soul to God" (p. 253). She encourages us to keep trying, and to experiment with different ways of praying. Julian experienced Jesus as a spouse offering companionship, even though she often felt unworthy. She felt God's love, light, warmth, and beauty penetrating her entire being. When we feel lonely and deprived of touch, we can share this with God. It is because of God's love that we are drawn to God, to be with God wholly loved. We come to realize that the only thing ultimately worth having is God. It is only through living in God that we can ultimately find peace.

Julian teaches us that the whole of life can be a prayer and that there is no "right" way to pray. She encourages us to find a way that suits our lifestyle while we are grieving over our divorce or separation. She reminds us that sometimes prayer will bring us immediate comfort, and sometimes prayer will be difficult and dry. God realizes this and is most pleased when we put time aside to pray, no matter how we are feeling.

And then our courteous Lord shows himself to the soul, happily and with the gladdest countenance, welcoming it as a friend, as if it had been in pain and in prison, saying: My dear darling, I am glad that you have come to me in all your woe. I have always been with you, and now you see me loving, and now we are made one in bliss (p. 246).

Suggested Activities

•Take some time to become completely still.

•Reread the passage from Luke of the woman anointing Jesus' feet with her tears. Imagine you are this woman. What story do your tears contain? Share this story with Jesus. Tell him how you feel. Allow him to touch the parts of you that are hurting so much. What does Jesus call you? What does his touch bring to you?

•Spend some time reading and reflecting on the imagery in the Song of Songs.

•Try to take special care of your body during your time of grieving, remembering that your body is good and beautiful, and that as Julian says there is an essential connection between our body and spirit. Make sure that you eat healthy food and get enough rest and exercise.

•Good friends can be honest with each other. Try to be emotionally honest with God about how you feel.

•During periods of grief, awareness of the senses changes. Sometimes they seem dulled; at other times they are more sensitive. Use each of the senses in prayer. Try to see in a new way. Listen to music, use incense or perfume, savor the food you eat, develop your sense of touch.

•An intimate relationship with God sometimes results in sexual feelings. Take time to nurture your sexuality and to be grateful for it, remembering that it is a precious gift from God.

•When you feel deprived of touch, ask a friend for a hug or have a massage.

•Experiment with some different ways of praying, such as centering prayer, dancing, singing, drawing, making a collage, working with clay, yoga, reflecting on images, or Tai Chi. Remember, however, not to make the method of prayer more important than the prayer itself.

Closing Prayer
And she came from behind,
broken and weeping.
She said nothing, yet you sensed her love.
You were able to share her sorrow,
to allow her tears to fall on your feet.
In that moment your feelings were united.

9

Confident Trust:
When God Seems Absent

Prayer can be difficult during the grieving process.

Opening Prayer
Nothingness.
Emptiness.
Aloneness.
I have lost all my familiar structures.
I feel I have nothing left.
Silence.
You seem absent.
Where are you, my God?
Sometimes I seem so alone.
You've left me;
I can't feel your presence.
Intellectually, I know you are near.
But now, O God, I desperately need
to sense your presence.
Teach me to be silent so that I may listen to you.
Steal in, the door is open.
Come, gentle breath of peace, I am yours.

The Word of God

While Jesus was on his way he could hardly breathe for the crowds. Among them was a woman who had suffered from hemorrhages for twelve years and nobody had been able to cure her. She came up from behind and touched the edge of his cloak, and at once her hemorrhage stopped. Jesus said, "Who was it who touched me?" All disclaimed it, and Peter said, "Master, the crowds are hemming in and pressing upon you!" But Jesus said, "Someone did touch me, for I felt the power had gone out of me." Then the woman seeing that she was detected, came trembling and fell at his feet. Before all the people she explained why she had touched him and how she had been cured instantly. He said to her, "Daughter, your faith has healed you. Go in peace" (Luke 8:42-48).

Reflection

This woman must have felt barren and lifeless because her bleeding drained all her energy and prevented her from giving birth. She never gave up hope, even though she must have felt God's absence in her life during her twelve years of ordeal. She shows us that we have to set time aside for prayer, even if we find that God does not come. Just to put some time aside and wait—that is all that matters. This woman was stigmatized as unclean. She was not only a woman, one of the poorest members of society, but also had been bleeding for a dozen years. She experienced rejection and humiliation for many years of her life.

She approached Jesus and touched him. In this touch she had an encounter with divine love, and her whole life became a prayer. She was then able to take responsibility for her own life, deciding to keep reaching out and trusting. By rethinking her position and being assertive, she broke the barriers imposed on her by society. Jesus turned her experience of bleeding around. She then came to recognize that the cross she was carrying was actually something that made her beautiful. She could understand that blood is a sacred fluid and can be a giver of life. It can be empowering. Rae and Marie Daly remind us:

> The power behind the experience of bleeding is that women are able to enter into the deep mysteries of life while learning to endure, to submit to the dark that is beyond conscious human control, and to learn that the way of life-giving, physically as well as spiritually, comes from within. Women know in the deep sense of knowing, not limited to the rationality of left brain discursive thought, that life and death are one, that there is a time to embrace and a time to let go. And they know that new life comes from within, not from without, transforming even as you are transformed, body from body in vibrant life connection.[11]

This woman encourages us to pray even when it seems difficult. She assures all women that God is active in our lives, even when life seems difficult. May we not lose hope—even though we may feel drained, lacking energy, and unable to trust—and reach out to discover God in new and unexpected places when God seems most absent.

Praying with Julian

Julian reminds us that even when we don't feel God's presence, God is there understanding our needs and appreciating all the efforts we make.

Julian's Wisdom

After this our Lord revealed about prayer, in which revelation I saw two conditions in our Lord's intention. One is rightful prayer; the other is confident trust. But still our trust is often not complete, because we are not sure that God hears us, as we think because of our unworthiness and because we are feeling nothing at all; for often we are as barren and dry after our prayers as we were before (p. 248).

Feeling barren and dry in prayer is a common experience that all spiritual classics mention. It is an experience that often comes up when we are grieving. We often want to give up praying because we are unable to express our sense of loss and outrage to God or to ourselves, and every time we try to pray we are faced with an avalanche of emotions we would prefer to forget, or we end up feeling dry nothingness. We may feel desperate loneliness and wonder if God is ever going to feel present to us. We may feel guilty at our anger and at a lack of trust in God. C.S. Lewis vividly describes the intensity of emotions during this time:

Meanwhile, where is God? This is one of the most disquieting symptoms. When you are happy, so happy that you have no sense of needing him, so happy that you are tempted to feel his claims upon you as an interruption; if you remember yourself and turn to him with gratitude and praise, you will be—or so it feels—welcomed with open arms. But go to him when your need is desperate, when all other help is in vain, and what do you find? A door slammed in your face, and a sound of bolting and double bolting on the inside. After that, silence. You may as well turn away. The longer you wait the more emphatic the silence will become. There are no lights in the windows. It might be an empty house. Was it ever inhabited? It seemed so once. And that seeming was as strong as this. What can this mean? Why is he so present a commander in our time of prosperity and so very absent in our time of trouble?[12]

This is a very common experience in a time of grief. Of course it is not God who closes the door but ourselves because we are so hurt we dare not risk to give any more. As panic, anger, outrage, hostility, a feeling of injustice, and resentment come up, these can be shared with God. When the woman touched Jesus, she was sharing her life experience with him. Jesus responded lovingly to her sharing. Julian also never lost hope in God. She experienced God's total trustworthiness. Julian also trusted that God could work through her, despite the limited expectations placed on women at that time. She reminds us to be honest with God about our feelings and to trust that our relationship with God will grow because of this experience.

Suggested Activities

•Take some time to reflect on the Scripture passage.

•Write on a piece of paper what you sense you need to let go of in order to move forward in your relationship with God. Burn this, offering this to God as the flames engulf it. Anoint yourself with perfume.

•Take a walk and scream out your feelings of anger. Tell God exactly how, what you feel. Remember that good friends can be honest about their feelings.

•Read through the passage from Luke again and reflect on

its contents. Talk to the woman with a hemorrhage and discover how she felt all the years she was rejected. What enabled her to rethink her position in life? What led to her become more assertive? What led her to trust and reach out to Jesus? Do you think you could do the same? The woman wanted to remain nameless and unrecognized but Jesus refused to allow her to remain invisible. He called her forth. Imagine now that Jesus is calling you forth. Remember that Jesus felt the woman's touch. Even our smallest efforts will be noticed.

•Perhaps you have had a previous difficult experience when you've felt pushed and pulled, or when God seemed absent. How were you called to conversion? Could you be called in the same way this time, or is this a very different experience?

•See if you can find some activities such as walking, swimming, gardening, or taking a bath that can become your prayer.

Closing Prayer

God, you are so totally trustworthy.
You are so surprisingly my gentle one.
I thought you would not accept my
anger and outrage.
I thought you had left me,
but now you are here listening.
Your presence is like a gentle breeze
drifting over my broken spirit.
I inhale you.
You, O God, are closer than the air I breathe.
You give me life.
You are my life.

10

Teach Me Your Ways, O God: Discernment While Grieving

We must seek discernment in making decisions.

Opening Prayer

Gentle one, loving one,
it is time to make decisions,
and yet I do not know what to do.
It's time to let go,
to step out of the world I used to know.
What choices should I make?
Bless these decisions, O God;
guide me in making them.

The Word of God

Meanwhile, a Samaritan woman came to draw water, and Jesus said to her, "Give me a drink." The woman said, "What! You a Jew ask for a drink from a Samaritan woman?" (Jews do not share drinking vessels with Samaritans.) Jesus replied: "If only you knew what God gives, and who it is that is asking you for a drink, you would have asked him and he would have given you living water." "Sir," the woman said, "you have no bucket and the well is deep, so where can you get 'living water'? Are you greater than Jacob our ancestor who gave us the well and drank from it himself, he and his sons and his cattle too?" Jesus answered, "Everyone who drinks this water will be thirsty again; but whoever drinks the water I shall give will never be thirsty again. The water that I shall give shall be a spring of water within, welling up and bringing eternal life." "Sir," said the woman, "give me this water, and then I shall not be thirsty, nor have to come all this way to draw water" (John 4:7-15).

Reflection

Jacob's well lay at a major crossroad, an apt place for an encounter between the woman and Jesus. The well became the site where a new direction was taken that irrevocably altered the destiny of the woman, who was grieving the many losses she had experienced in her relationships, which had scarred her. She had come to this sacred place to collect water, perhaps because she was aware that it was Jacob's well and it would be a kind of pilgrimage for her. She was no doubt surprised that Jesus would speak with her because she was a woman and a Samaritan. Samaritans were discriminated against and custom did not allow a rabbi to speak to a woman. It was also quite unorthodox for Jesus to drink from the same jar as the woman. Jesus openly accepted her and she was delighted by this. At first, she did not understand Jesus asking her for a drink, and she interpreted the ensuing conversation about the water literally. She then listened deeply to Jesus' message and tapped the meaning of what he was saying. Jesus was referring to "living water" and spiritual thirst. A relationship with the Jesus who would suffer could quench her spiritual thirst.

In the encounter the woman came to see which direction her life would take. She was moved to her decision because she recognized that Jesus understood her. It was as if he held a mirror to her face. She felt mutual respect and understanding. They challenged each other. She had listened to Jesus in a contemplative way and would know how to make a decision that would honor God's will.

Grieving creates a sense of confusion, anxiety, restlessness, and an inability to make sound decisions. It is a time when we need help to perceive issues clearly. We need spiritual support at such a time—nourished by the living water of Jesus—so that we can make wise decisions. Ignatius, the master of discernment, wisely reminds us never to change a decision while we are in turmoil or depressed or discouraged,[13] and yet so often in the initial stages of separation or divorce many decisions must be made: about housing, a new career, children's needs, and finances. Making all these decisions can be overwhelming. If we get in touch with the "living water" that Jesus offers, we can catch an insight in our hearts into what is true and wise for us. Like the woman at the well, we are challenged to make decisions that direct us toward God.

Praying with Julian

Julian teaches us how to rely on our spiritual supports. She, like the woman at the well, knew what it was like to receive Jesus' living water. She teaches us always to go to Jesus for guidance if we are to act wisely. When we do this, she reassures us that all will be well.

Julian's Wisdom

And then I was answered in my reason, as it were by a friendly intermediary: Accept it generally, and contem-

plate the courtesy of your Lord God as he revealed it to
you, for it is more honor to God to contemplate him in all
things than in any one special thing....And if I were to act
wisely, in accordance with this teaching, I should not be
glad because of any special thing or be greatly distressed
by anything at all, for all will be well; for the fullness of
joy is to contemplate God in everything (pp. 236-237).

Julian knows that God will help us discern what the right
decision is so that all will be well. She teaches us to take all our
worries to Jesus who will enable us to stop worrying and to
contemplate God in all things. It is God's intention that we enjoy life. God is in all things, so God is certainly with us when
we make decisions.

Suggested Activities
•Take some time to become completely still.
    •Like the woman at the well, dialogue with Jesus about
your concerns. List the decisions you have to make and pri-
oritize them. See if there are some you can let go of until you
feel stronger.
    •Now take the most pressing decision. Choose two colors.
Paint a picture to represent one choice with the first color.
Then paint the other choice with the second. Which seems to
bring most peace and freedom? Remember that God speaks
only in peace and gentleness.
    •Again, take this matter back to Jesus. Tell him how you
feel about it. Remember that making the better choice may be
difficult, but you always have a loving God who will help you.
Set a time limit on when you will finally make your decision.
    •Keep in mind that whenever we make a good decision that
comes from God, there will sometimes be a negative response.

Ask God to help you to listen, and respond only to the good spirit.

Closing Prayer

My God, my creator, my lover,
please help me to choose a direction
that will bring growth and life.
May I always remember
that all will be well,
even when life does not turn out the way I expect.
Guide my decisions.

11

Claiming Our Power

We are called not to passive submission, but to freedom, creativity, and new life.

Opening Prayer
Power seems such a negative word,
yet it is really your gift to me, O God.
Teach me to be powerful—
and humble
and peaceful.
Give me courage.

The Word of God

[Jesus] moved on from there into the territory of Tyre. He found a house to stay in, and would like to have remained unrecognized, but that was impossible. Almost at once a woman whose small daughter was possessed by an unclean spirit heard of him and came and fell at his feet. (The woman was a Gentile, a Phoenician of Syria by nationality.) She begged him to drive the demon out of her daughter. He said to her, "Let the children be satisfied first; it is not right to take the children's bread and throw it to the dogs." "Sir," she replied, "even the dogs under the table eat the children's scraps." He said to her, "For saying that, go, and you will find that the de-

---

mon has left your daughter." And when she returned home, she found the child lying in bed. The demon had left her (Mark 7:24-30).

Reflection

This woman portrayed in Mark's gospel had the confidence to reply to Jesus. She felt she had rights and was prepared to speak up for them. She uses her power for the benefit of another, since she was concerned about her daughter, one of the most powerless members of society. She responded to Jesus so that someone who was weak could be empowered. We are not to be afraid, she teaches us, to express how we really feel and to dialogue with Jesus honestly and openly.

Separation and divorce can be a lonely, frightening time, which engenders feelings of passivity. We often feel we are powerless. As we begin to take charge of our lives, we begin to realize that it is "powerlessness, not power that corrupts our lives and our dreams."[14] Owning feelings of passivity can lead to an openness to the presence of the divine in the experience and imagination of women. Being honest about who we are will result in an inner and outer freedom. We come to realize that our compassionate God does not wish humans to suffer, but longs for justice. God is on the side of poor, broken women, gently calling us to fullness of life. God actively empowers women, drives out their fears, and gives them new faith and the courage to risk speaking and acting in the name of those who have no power.

Praying with Julian

Julian also teaches us to have confidence in who we are as women so that we may become agents for change in our society. She embodies for us the fact that our experience of brokenness is a gift that exposes our deep and total dependence on God. The result of this gift is a realization that we have a responsibility to love all who are powerless, to denounce anything in society that creates oppression and alienation, and to promote dignity, freedom, mutuality, peace, and justice for all.

Julian's Wisdom

And verily and truly he will manifest to us all this marvelous joy when we shall see him. And our good Lord wants us to believe this and trust, rejoice and delight, strengthen and console ourselves, as we can with his grace and with his help, until the time when we see it in reality (p. 189).

For truly I saw and understood in our Lord's meaning that he revealed it because he wants to have it better known than it is. In which knowledge he wants to give us grace to love him and to cleave to him, for he beholds his heavenly treasure with so great love on earth that he will give us more light and solace in heavenly joy, by drawing our hearts from the sorrow and darkness which we are in.

And from the time that it was revealed, I desired many times to know in what was our Lord's meaning. And fifteen years after and more, I was answered in spiritual understanding, and it was said: What, do you wish to know your Lord's meaning in this thing? Know it well, love was his meaning. Who reveals it to you? Love. What did he reveal to you? Love. Why does he reveal it to you? For love. Remain in this, and you will know more of the same (p. 342).

Julian's words echo John 15:9: "...dwell in my love." When we dwell in God's love we have power, power from God, power to be our true selves. Julian assures us that it is only in entering the struggle of taking the journey with Jesus that we will ever find true joy and divine empowerment.

Suggested Activities

• Take some time to become completely still.

• List the qualities of the Phoenician woman that you admire.

• Reflect on your family history and see if there is someone in your family who offers you a healthy model of power.

• See if you can remember a time when it was right for you to be assertive. Can you name what enabled you to be so?

• Reflect on times when you have felt dependent rather than independent. What supports can you use that will enable you to become more independent?

• Choose an image that gives insight into the powerful part of yourself. Reflect on your feelings about this image. Now think about the times when you seem most powerless. Find an image to describe this. Again, reflect on your feelings. Hold this image gently, seeing if you can imagine a time when an awareness of this powerlessness will become one of your greatest gifts.

• Say the words from John's gospel, "Dwell in my love," over and over as a mantra.

Closing Prayer

Beloved God, who gently calls me to be myself,
hold me, surround me in your love
as you teach me to let go
of past ways of knowing.

Teach me to be proud of my past,
to see your love reflected in it,
even when I don't recognize you.
It is now my turn to take the initiative,
to be Woman reflecting your goodness.
Teach me gratefulness.
Teach me wisdom.
Teach me to empower others.
Teach me to reach out and take risks
in your name.

12

Living Life Playfully Again

We are called to embrace womankind and discover the sacred within so that we come to a deeper understanding of self as sacred presence.

Opening Prayer
O God,
I have received the gift of weeping
and have wept for so long.
Now it is time to dry my eyes.
Now my sorrow has turned into joy.
Now I am beginning to flower again.

The Word of God
Jesus was at Bethany in the house of Simon the leper; he was at dinner when a woman came in with an alabaster jar of costly ointment, pure nard. She broke the jar and poured the ointment on his head. Some who were there said to one another indignantly, "Why this waste of ointment? Ointment like this could have been sold for over three hundred denarii and the money given to the poor"; and they were angry with her. But Jesus said, "Leave her alone. Why are you upsetting her? What she has done for me is one of the good works. You have the poor with you always, and you can be kind to them whenever

you wish, but you will not always have me. She has done what was in her power to do: she has anointed my body beforehand for its burial. I tell you solemnly, wherever throughout the world the good news is proclaimed, what she has done will be told also in memory of her (Mark 14:3-9).

Reflection
This is a significant story about a woman who has wisdom and power. She is wise enough to recognize Jesus as the Christ, one who should be anointed, and she has courage enough to anoint him in front of his would-be critics. Her anointing nurtured him for the next part of his journey. This woman was truly herself, being playful and joyful and appreciating the gifts of life. She was flowering. She was able to offer her gifts to empower others, and Jesus wanted her remembered for this. She encourages us to flower, to acknowledge and to use our gifts, to stand up to do what we are persuaded we should do, and to be women of love.

Praying with Julian
Julian was also a woman who was flowering. She too was able to share her gifts and to empower others. She could do this because she had suffered and had shared her suffering with Jesus. She had spent an appropriate time undertaking the tasks of grieving. After fifteen years of reflecting on the meaning of her Showings, she decided to share her wisdom with "all her ever Christians." Toward the end of her Showing she explains that the whole reason we exist is for love; we are surrounded by the love of God and are called to rejoice in this with God.

Julian's Wisdom
And with this our good Lord said most joyfully: See how

I love you, as if he had said, my darling, behold and see your Lord, your God, who is your Creator and your endless joy; see your own brother, your savior; my child, behold and see what delight and bliss I have in your salvation, and for my love rejoice with me.

And for my greater understanding, these blessed words were said: See how I love you, as if he had said, behold and see that I loved you so much, before I died for you, that I wanted to die for you. And now I have died for you, and willingly suffered what I could. And now all my bitter pain and my hard labor is turned into everlasting joy and bliss for me and for you. How could it now be that you would pray for me for anything pleasing to me which I would not gladly grant to you? For my delight is in your holiness and in your endless joy and bliss in me (p. 221).

Finally, the cycle of grief becomes shorter and healing takes place. This can bring new challenges to see the suffering as gift and to use this period of grieving to support and encourage others who are undergoing the same experience. Now we are being called to flower and to become sacred symbols, signs of God to the world.

Suggested Activities
•Compose yourself in peace and become completely still.

•Choose a painting of a woman you like. You may find this in an art book or on a calendar or postcard, or at the art gallery. Choose something that symbolizes the flowering of women. Look at this picture, seeing its power, energy, and beauty. Notice the sensuality and sensitivity, the simplicity and elegance. View it from a variety of angles. Touch it and allow it to speak to you. Look for sharp lines, graceful lines, and choose a line or a shape that speaks to you. Stay with the picture for a while. Reflect on its colors. Move into the painting itself. How does it feel? What does it remind you of? As you become absorbed in the painting, reflect on what it is saying to you.

•Draw your response on a piece of paper, noting whether you are being led out of the security and comfort of the picture to meet the world.

•Is the painting caressing you, nurturing you?

•What does this picture say to you about the grieving process?

•Can you recognize some ways in which you are beginning to flower again as a woman? List these.

•Are there some interests that you enjoy such as going to the art gallery, the theater, or a movie that will add joy and richness to your life? Try to make time to nurture yourself in this way.

Closing Prayer
Healing God,
now I am called to cease my weeping.
I can now appreciate my suffering as gift.
Help me to support others who are grieving.
Nourish me as I take risks
to trust
to love
to flower again.

Notes

1. All quotations are taken from Edmund Colledge and James Walsh, *Julian of Norwich: Showings* (New York: Paulist Press, 1978).

2. For more details, see B. Pelphrey, *Julian of Norwich* (Wilmington, Del.: Michael Glazier, 1989), pp. 235-248.

3. All scripture quotes are from *The Jerusalem Bible* (Garden City, N.Y.: Doubleday, 1966).

4. Adapted from Maria Harris, *Dance of the Spirit: The Seven Steps of Women's Spirituality* (New York: Bantam, 1991).

5. Elizabeth Obbard, "God Alone Suffices" in Robert Llewellyn (ed.), *Julian: Woman of Our Day* (Mystic, Conn.: Twenty-Third Publications, 1985), p. 110.

6. Pelphrey, *Julian of Norwich*, p. 68.

7. Kathleen Fischer, *The Inner Rainbow* (Mahwah, N.J.: Paulist Press, 1983), p. 92.

8. W. Bridges, *Transitions: Making Sense of Life's Changes* (Reading, Mass.: Addison Wesley, 1980), p. 94.

9. F. Nemeck and M. Coombs, *Contemplation* (Wilmington, Del.: Michael Glazier, 1982), p. 23.

10. Taken from a lecture given in New York in 1987.

11. Rae and Marie Daly, *Created in Her Image* (New York: Crossroad, 1990), p. 50.

12. C.S. Lewis, *A Grief Observed* (New York: Bantam Books, 1980), p. 4.

13. Thomas Greene, S.J., *Weeds Among the Wheat* (Notre Dame, Ind.: Ave Maria Press, 1986), pp. 107-108.

14. Harris, *Dance of the Spirit*, p. 37.

Of Related Interest...

Women of the Gospel
Sharing God's Compassion
Isaias Powers, CP

Readers meet 28 women of the Gospels being sent from heaven to bring God's compassion to those in need on earth. 168 pp, $5.95

WomanStory
Biblical Models for Our Time
Sister Pamela Smith, SS.C.M.
with art by Sister Virginia DeWan, SS.C.M.

Each of the 56 chapters features a woman from the Bible and uses Scripture passages and reflections to show her relationship with her God and with her people. 112 pp, $7.95

From Worry to Wellness
21 People Who Changed Their Lives
Ruth Morrison and Dawn Radtke

These stories offer positive and practical ways to change for the better, based on real-life examples. 192 pp, $7.95

Facing Depression
Toward Healing the Mind, Body & Spirit
Michael Lawson

The author uses actual experiences to illustrate the many faces and forms of depression, and highlights biblical passages to provide encouragement. 160 pp, $7.95

Healing Wounded Emotions
Overcoming Life's Hurts
Martin Padovani

This book describes how our emotional and spiritual lives interact, and challenges readers to live fuller, more satisfying lives. 128 pp, $6.95

Available at religious bookstores or from
TWENTY-THIRD PUBLICATIONS
P.O. Box 180 • Mystic, CT 06355 • 1-800-321-0411